# Animals at PLAY

by K. M. Kostyal

Two playful tiger cubs roll around in the grass.

BOOKS FOR YOUNG EXPLORERS
NATIONAL GEOGRAPHIC SOCIETY

Do you like to play in the snow? Snow flies as a young wolf leaps and pounces. A soft landing in deep snow is fun. A lot of animals play, just as you do, for the fun of it.

Animals often play all alone.
A baby baboon does a somersault
and looks at the world upside down.
This young brown bear has been playing
in the first snowfall. He used his nose
like a little plow to dig in the snow.
Soon he will curl up in his cozy den
for his winter sleep.

4

Before they are old enough to play with each other, baby animals often play with their parents. A lioness lets cubs crawl on her and bite her gently. One curious cub even puts its paw in a lioness's mouth. She will be gentle and will not hurt the cub. Sometimes a lioness catches a cub by the tail and tugs it playfully.

As the lion cubs grow older, they play more often with each other. A swat with a paw may mean "Let's play!"

They nip and paw each other
and tumble around on the ground.
Wrestling is fun for these cubs
and for other young animals.
Have you ever watched puppies
or kittens play-fight like this?

When animals are having fun, they make a happy play face. The baby chimpanzee hanging from a branch seems to have a smile on his face. His mother is tickling his tummy.

These Alaska brown bears are wrestling in the water. Are they playing or fighting? You can tell by looking at their faces. They seem to be smiling at each other. Playing helps them stay friends.

Foxes ask each other to play by making
a play bow. Dogs and wolves do this, too.
They stretch out their front legs and bow down.
They open their mouths. Then they play-fight.
Playing like this helps them grow strong.

If one fox wants to stop and rest, it rolls over
on its back and looks up at the other one.

**W**hen kangaroos play-fight, they look like dancers. They stand straight up and push and kick, but they almost never hurt each other.

Young seals play-fight, too. They bite and push each other, as grown-up males do when they fight.

Do you ever play tag with your friends? Animals chase one another, too. This big dog is running slowly down the beach so his little friend can keep up with him.

Fawns race through the fields and forests where they live. Running helps make their legs strong. As they grow, the deer will run faster and faster.

A polar bear floating in his pool at the zoo has a barrel for a toy. He bats it around. Sometimes he throws it in the water, then chases after it.

Animals often play with things they find around them. A chimpanzee at the zoo kicks and swats a sack. The chimpanzee's face tells you that this animal is having fun.

Two puppies are playing tug-of-war with a sock. GRRRR! Which puppy do you think will get the sock?

In a high, rocky desert, a mother
mountain lion meets a tortoise moving
slowly along. She catches it and shows it
to her two cubs. They play with it,
rolling it around and pouncing on it.
Someday they may hunt tortoises to eat.

These fur seals are riding the waves in the ocean. They use their bodies as surfboards. They get on top of a wave and let it carry them in to shore.

**M**any young animals play together
the way you and your friends do.
On a sandy beach, three golden retriever
puppies seem to be playing follow-the-leader.

A tree trunk is a good place for chimpanzees
in Africa to play ring-around-the-rosy.
Wild lambs bump heads for fun as they stand
on a steep mountain slope in Alaska.

These small African antelopes are called springboks. They can spring straight up in the air, as if jumping for joy. Sometimes they jump like this as a signal that danger is near.

Mountain goat kids push each other with their heads. Who is king of the castle?

29

Orangutan playmates have been running and chasing and climbing. They found some twigs to chew on. They have had a lot of fun. Now it's time to rest.

After splashing and playing in a river, a brown bear lies down and cools off.

*Cover:* A terrier named Pippin looks ready to play.

Published by
The National Geographic Society, Washington, D.C.
Gilbert M. Grosvenor, *President and Chairman of the Board*
Melvin M. Payne, Thomas W. McKnew, *Chairmen Emeritus*
Owen R. Anderson, *Executive Vice President*
Robert L. Breeden, *Senior Vice President,*
  *Publications and Educational Media*

Prepared by
The Special Publications and School Services Division
Donald J. Crump, *Director*
Philip B. Silcott, *Associate Director*
Bonnie S. Lawrence, *Assistant Director*

Staff for this book
Jane H. Buxton, *Managing Editor*
Charles E. Herron, *Illustrations Editor*
Viviane Y. Silverman, *Art Director*
Peggy D. Winston, *Researcher*
Artemis S. Lampathakis, *Illustrations Assistant*
Marisa J. Farabelli, Rosamund Garner, Kaylene Kahler,
  Sandra F. Lotterman, Eliza C. Morton, Dru McLoud
  Stancampiano, *Staff Assistants*

Engraving, Printing, and Product Manufacture
George V. White, *Director, Manufacturing and*
  *Quality Management*
Vincent P. Ryan, *Manager, Manufacturing and*
  *Quality Management*
David V. Showers, *Production Manager*
Kathleen M. Cirucci, *Production Project Manager*
Carol R. Curtis, *Senior Production Staff Assistant*

Consultants
Dr. Robert Fagen, University of Alaska, and Dr. Ronald M.
  Nowak, U. S. Department of the Interior,
  *Scientific Consultants*
Dr. Ine N. Noe, *Educational Consultant*
Dr. Lynda Bush, *Reading Consultant*

Illustrations Credits
Tony Stone Worldwide/Masterfile (cover); Alan D. Carey (1); © Jim Bran-
denburg (2-3, 24-25); Timothy W. Ransom, Ph.D. (4); © Kathy Dawson (4-5);
Jen and Des Bartlett (6-7 all, 28-29); K. Amman/Bruce Coleman Inc. (8); Carl
Purcell (8-9, 16-17 upper); Hugo van Lawick (10); Tom Walker (11, 13 lower,
26 lower); Stephen J. Krasemann/DRK PHOTO (12-13 upper; 22, 23 upper);
Toni Angermayer/Photo Researchers, Inc. (14); Frank S. Balthis (15); Tom
and Pat Leeson (17 lower); Animals Animals/M. Austerman (18-19); Animals Animals/J. C. Stevenson (20); Julie Habel/West Light (20-21); Steven J.
Krasemann/Photo Researchers, Inc. (23 lower); Hiroe K. Keeler (26-27 upper); Jane Goodall (27 right); Charles G. Summers, Jr. (29 right); Bob Wavra
(30-31); Tom Bledsoe/Photo Researchers, Inc. (32).

**Library of Congress CIP Data**
Kostyal, K. M., 1951-
  Animals at play.
  (Books for young explorers)
  Bibliography: p.
  Summary: Discusses the way in which a variety of animals play, including
the baboon, brown bear, and fox.
  1. Play behavior in animals—Juvenile literature.   [1. Play behavior in
animals. 2. Animals—Habits and behavior]   I. Title.   II. Series.
QL763.5.K67   1988                    599′.051                    88-15209
ISBN 0-87044-739-4 (regular edition)
ISBN 0-87044-744-0 (library edition)

# MORE ABOUT Animals at Play

We know when we're playing, but just what is play? Whether it is blowing bubbles, making a sand castle, playing touch football with cousins before a holiday dinner, or throwing a stick for a puppy to fetch, play is something we do for its own sake, just because it is fun. And when the puppy fetches the stick, it is playing, too.

Researchers have been studying the play behavior of animals for years; they now realize that animals play for the same reasons we do—because it feels good. Animals may play in the snow (2-3, 4-5)* or spring into the air (28-29) or even tickle each other (10).

Play is important to the development of both animals and humans.

When the young play, they explore their world and practice the skills they will need to survive. The exercise they get when they leap and roll and run helps develop their bodies. The young baboon doing somersaults (4) is testing her agility and sense of balance, and she is seeing what the world looks like upside down. Anyone who has ever done a somersault knows how much fun it is to make everything go topsy-turvy.

Animals have many ways of letting each other know they want to play. Dogs, foxes, and wolves make a play bow (12-13). Tigers, lions, and other kinds of cats swat and push (1, 8-9). One signal that is shared by dozens of different species is the play face (10, 11), a relaxed, open-mouthed grin that means "I'm having fun."

When two animals are tussling, their faces may tell you if they're play-fighting. The ears of some animals, like bears and cats, may also reflect their mood. Ears pointing up or turned forward may signal that the animal is having fun. On the other hand, an animal with its ears flattened may be in an aggressive mood, and its play is becoming serious business.

When animals play-fight, they usually do not hurt each other. Cats, for example, may retract their claws. When playing animals nip at each other, they can bite without using the full force of their jaws. Often when they wrestle, some

*Numbers in parentheses refer to pages in *Animals at Play*.

ANN FREDERICK PURCELL

A cat swats at the bell on a dog's collar, but the dog doesn't seem to mind. Pet animals often enjoy playing with each other. Sometimes even wild animals of different species play together. Ravens may pester a wolf by diving at its head or pecking its tail. If the wolf snaps at them, they jump aside, then swoop back to tease it again.

kinds of animals take turns being dominant and submissive. One animal takes the belly-up, or submissive, position (13) for a while, lying on its back with its legs in the air; the other animal assumes the dominant posture over it. Then the play-wrestlers may reverse positions and start again.

Play-fighting helps young animals develop muscle coordination and skills. Wild lambs and kids on a steep slope butting heads (26, 29) are practicing their natural sure-footedness. This experience will help them when they must fight with members of their own species or face a predator.

For wild animals that live in groups, such as wolves and lions, playing together helps to build friendships. Such friendships, or social bonds, can help the animals survive. They practice compromise and cooperation in "games" such as ring-around-the-rosy (27) or king-of-the-castle (29). As they play, the animals interact with objects and with features of their landscape, as well as with other members of their group.

Animals often play alone or with an object such as a leaf or a string (cover, 20-21). Sometimes the object turns out to be part of something bigger—like their mother's tail or their human companion's fingers. Puppies may even chase their own tails. Playing with objects rehearses movements and skills that adult animals use for survival. You have probably seen kittens crouching and watching an object, then stalking it and suddenly pouncing. They are using the gestures of adult cats hunting prey.

Play has risks as well as benefits. An animal may injure itself, or it may be so engrossed in play that it does not notice the approach of a predator. Play may cost an animal energy it needs for survival. In harsh environments, where survival is difficult, animals tend to conserve their energy more and play less. Regardless of the risks involved, play seems to be a vital part of growing up for many mammals.

Interestingly, mammals and birds are the most playful of animals. They are also the most intelligent. Fish, reptiles, and amphibians play rarely, if at all.

Birds dart after each other and play with objects. They also play with other animals. A raven may tease a wolf by swooping down so low that the wolf leaps for it. Chimpanzees and baboons play together, too, as do cats and dogs, and humans and their pets.

In their play, young animals often mimic adult behavior. Young male elephant seals nipping and lunging at each other are imitating the gestures that adult males make when defending their harems (15).

The earliest and most enduring kinds of play are between parents and offspring and between siblings. A mother chimpanzee tickles her baby (10), and two lion cubs tussle (8-9). Can you and your children find other examples of family play in this book?

Here are some other activities that might help your children learn more about animals at play:

Watch kittens playing together. Do they make any sounds when they tussle? Look at their paws. Can you see the claws? Sometimes kittens retract their claws when they play.

Go to a nearby playground or park where people walk their dogs, and watch the dogs greet each other. Do they invite each other to play?

If you have a puppy for a pet or if you know one in your neighborhood, try asking it to play by making the play bow yourself: Get down on your knees, then lean forward with your chest almost touching the floor and your arms straight out. Your friend will probably be excited to find out you know how to communicate with it in its own language. (Never play with dogs or cats that you do not know. They may be dangerous.)

Visiting a zoo or an animal park is a good way to have fun and to learn the different ways that animals play. Which animals are the most playful? Find out which animals have young. Observe how mothers and their young play together.

Think of all the things you do to have fun, whether it's just lying in the grass daydreaming, or digging your toes in soft, warm sand, or playing ball with your friends. What do you enjoy the most?

# Additional Reading

*Animal Play Behavior,* by Robert Fagen. (N.Y., Oxford University Press, 1981). Scholarly reference.

*Animals At Play,* by Laurence Pringle. (N.Y., Harcourt Brace Jovanovich, 1985). Ages 8-12.

*Book of Mammals,* 2 vols. (Washington, D.C., National Geographic Society, 1981). Ages 8 and up.

*My Life with the Chimpanzees,* by Jane Goodall. (N.Y., Minstrel/Pocket Books, 1988). Ages 8-16.

*Play,* by Catherine Garvey. (Cambridge, Mass., Harvard University Press, 1977). Adults.